How to Live Happily Married: for Engaged Couples

Top 15 Discussions You Need to Have Before the Wedding for a Strong Relationship

By: Daisy Diamante

WOOLLEY

Table of Contents:

FREE GIFT!

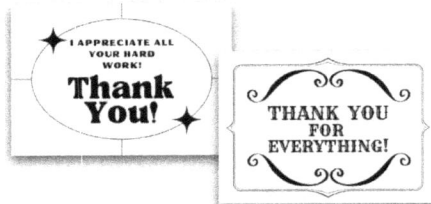

Gratitude Cards!

*Give to those you appreciate: spouse, family, friends, co-workers, a helpful employee, etc...
*Includes pdf pages with 16 cards: 8 black & white and 8 in color, allowing you to choose your desired ink preference while printing.
*Super Convenient! The standard credit card size makes them easy to carry and readily accessible!
*Print on photo paper for a more sturdy card.
*Be creative! Personalize them by writing a note on the back! Surprise someone & make their day!

http://freegift.woolleypublishing.com

DEDICATION:

Thank you to my wonderful husband & collaborator, my amazing extended family, friends, & God for all of life's blessings!

Happy 40th Anniversary
to my incredible parents!

Thank you for being an inspiration to us all! May everyone be blessed to have a Marriage as strong and happy as yours!

Introduction:

Congratulations! You have promised to marry someone you love! This is such an exciting time in your life! This book will ensure communication and confidence in your relationship as you move forward!

Throughout this book, I refer to couples as partners. You ARE creating a partnership! You are a team with the person whom you love! This bond should be based on trust and understanding. When you and your partner say, "I do," you will commit to teamwork for a lifetime - not just for one day.

Weddings are a special day - but still just one day. Near or far, large or small, the Wedding Day is the important date you officially make a lifelong commitment to someone who means the world to you. Marriage is the maintenance of that commitment. It requires daily cooperation and hard work. It isn't always easy, but it is worth it! This book is to help you and your partner make sure you are ready for this life-long commitment. The questions in this book are meant to be answered together- honestly and openly. Spark conversations that will help solidify your relationship before saying, "I DO!"

The questions in Section One are to be answered as soon as possible and honestly! Some of the questions may be uncomfortable, but they ARE necessary. If you both already know the answers, still go through it together and then give your partner a high five that you are off to a great start!

Sections Two through Five can always be answered as Newlyweds, as it has more fun and conversational probing questions. Section One, however, needs to be answered NOW! Grab your future spouse! Ready? Set - **GO!**

Section One:

15 Important Discussions Before the Wedding!

<u>Do NOT Marry without Knowing & Accepting the Answers to these Questions!</u>

#1

Why do you want to get married, and why this particular person?

What does marriage mean to you? Are you only getting married to have the 'big day,' or are you eager to spend your life with this person?

Likewise, what do you love about your person? Make sure it's not their looks alone - you will still be seeing this person naked in forty-plus years. Even if they have your idea of the 'perfect body' now, life does happen, and people change - both physically and emotionally. Will you still love this person with those changes? Make sure you are not marrying for money either. Marriage is supposed to be 'for richer, for poorer.' If your partner is wealthy now, that can change from unexpected life events such as a job loss, medical issues, gambling/ excessive splurging, etc... While living on a budget can be difficult, make sure you love this person enough to do whatever it takes to make it through the tough times you may experience together.

#2

How well do you know your future spouse, and do they really know you?

If you've promised to spend forever with this person, you should already know the answers to these questions:

What makes you laugh hysterically?

What don't you like to be teased about?

What puts you in a horrible mood? Fantastic mood?

What makes you feel vulnerable? How can your partner help you when you encounter this?

What brings you joy?

What are your fears?

What's something most people don't know about you that your partner already knows?

Is there something you've always wanted to ask your partner but haven't? (Now is the time!)

_____

_____

_____

#3

What do you want your family unit to look like? Do you want children? How about pets?

This is a significant topic that NEEDS to be discussed before you go any further! This is something very personal on both sides of the coin. You will NOT change your partner's mind - nor should you want to! This is where respect and honesty come into play. You should respect your partner enough to want their happiness, but not for the sake of yours! If one of you wants to be a parent and the other doesn't, it will cause conflict when the time comes. It will also affect the parenting process and, subsequently, the child's emotional well-being. This is a decision that needs to be made TOGETHER. Make sure you are both on the same page. whichever choice.

(If your partner has children already, this marriage makes YOU a parent. You are joining a family unit and need to make sure you are comfortable with this and willing to compromise! If you are already plotting how to *treat the child or get rid of them like an evil stepparent or scheming against your partner's ex, you NEED to reevaluate your life and consider ending the engagement. Talk to your future spouse about your feelings - NOW!)*

Likewise, are you a cat person, a dog person, or a - something else person? If a cat person marries a dog person, thinking they will convince them never to get another dog - think again! If you dislike dogs and your partner wants a dog to always be in their life (or snakes, or...), it will cause resentment on either side. Discuss your expectations on what your entire family unit will consist of.

_____

_____

_____

_____

_____

_____

_____

_____

_____

_____

Bonus Information: Tokophobia

Have you heard of "Tokophobia?" If not, it is a relatively new term introduced in 2000 by The British Journal of Psychiatry and was included in the 2015 ICD (International Classification of Disease). (Tocophobia [Tokophobaia]: What is it and how to treat this, 2018).

So what is tokophobia? It's the fear of pregnancy and/ or childbirth. There are two main divisions of tokophobia: primary (those who have never given birth) and secondary (those who have already been pregnant and/ or given birth.)

Tokophobia isn't as simple as just being afraid of the labor pain (though that can be a contributing factor.) For some with primary tokophobia, the very thought of feeling the baby growing inside them makes them think of horror films (such as 2020s The Expecting) rather than the maternal warmth and joy women typically feel. For others, negative stories and experiences with raising children may have created an anxiety-filled fear of ever becoming pregnant. These women will often want to use multiple forms of birth control with their partners. The passionate afterglow they experience is replaced by waves of anxiety, stress, and fear for the remainder of the month - until they get their menstrual period and can breathe once again. Many will even take multiple pregnancy tests to ease their anxiety, despite how many forms of birth control were used.

Women with secondary tokophobia may have experienced a difficult pregnancy or labor involved (even postpartum depression), and they don't want to relive the experience. Like women with primary tokophobia, they will insist on multiple forms of birth control or even abstain from sexual intercourse altogether if the fear is strong enough to outweigh the passion and love for their partner.

What does this mean for the newly engaged? Honesty! If primary or secondary tokophobia resembles your own feelings, know that you are not alone. Discuss your feelings with your future spouse and/ or a professional. You and your partner need to decide if having a family is equally something you both want (or don't want). If you do, there are options like surrogacy or adoption to consider. If children aren't part of the family unit you envision, consider (and openly discuss as a couple) options like a vasectomy or hysterectomy.

Most importantly, you and your partner are a team! Be on the same page, create a game plan, and ignore the noise coming from the stands. Your life is your game, so play it your way!

#4

What did your family think of your partner when they first met? What did you think of your future in-laws? How about now?

Families can be complicated and unique, to put it simply. Your expectations in joining two families together are essential to discuss with your future spouse. You and your spouse need to be open and honest about how you feel about the other's family. Not everyone needs to agree or get along, but you need to know how your partner truly feels and how the feelings are reciprocated. This will prepare you both for future drama that inevitably happens amongst families.

_____

_____

_____

_____

_____

_____

_____

#5

What are your expectations for the holidays and other celebrations?

Just as the type of Wedding you have should be a mutual decision, so should future holidays and other celebrations. Is there a favorite holiday or tradition held by one family necessary to continue? Agree and discuss with your families if the holidays will be split up, or you can start to include your partner's side with your family's events (and vice versa.) It is important to create an agreed game plan now, especially before children become involved. While alternating holidays can work for some families, there may be resentment during a side's 'off-year.' This is why these expectations are essential to set up now.

Maybe you both want to create new traditions and host holidays and celebrations yourselves? What exactly does 'entertaining' mean to both of you? Will you have an elegant formal dinner? Will it be laid back with pajamas, pizza, and popcorn? Both are great - as long as you agree. If hosting a perfect, elegant holiday dinner stresses one of you out, there will be resentment and frustration every year when that time comes around. Discuss now what ideal holiday plans look like and how you wish to celebrate.

_____

_____

_____

_____

_____

_____

_____

_____

_____

_____

_____

_____

_____

_____

_____

_____

_____

_____

_____

#6

Where do your religious and political beliefs align? Can you peacefully agree to disagree with your partner on any differences?

Religion and politics are topics that people try to avoid with the general public. It makes adults "cranky" (my young cousin's excellent adjective) and causes conflicts when there are differences of opinion. However, since your partner is someone you are spending your life with, you need to have these discussions & **accept** those differences. If you choose to have children, consider what religion (and other beliefs) you will raise them to have.

Also, how does your partner react to the differences of others? If they begin arguments with others over religion or politics at any social function, they will continue to do so. Make sure you are accepting and understanding of that.   If you like to be argumentative too, great - you are on the same page! However, when both of you need to be correct *and want to be enthusiastically persuasive, you may not be invited to many social gatherings. (A personal favorite phrase of mine, "avoiding a fight is a mark of* honor; only fools insist on quarreling.") (Bible Hub, *Proverb20:3.)*

_____

_____

_____

_____

_____

_____

_____

_____

_____

_____

_____

_____

_____

_____

_____

_____

#7

What does 'success' mean to you? What do you want most out of life? How would you describe your saving & spending habits? Does either of you have debt? What's your savings goal?

It is essential to discuss finances and future goals with your partner. You want both of your lives to be successful, so make sure your definitions of success align. If one person defines success as having a mansion with lots of luxuries and another person sees success as living debt-free in a modest home, the first will never be truly happy with the second person.

Also, be sure to have an in-depth discussion on finances with your partner. Even if there is one income providing for the family unit, make sure you both know the income and financial expectations. Any issues of debt should be discussed with your partner. This will cause problems when trying to purchase a car or a *home. You both need to be upfront and honest with each other. Also, decide if you will be setting up joint checking or savings accounts.*

It is also imperative to discuss how you will be saving for your shared future. Sit down and discuss your savings strategy. Create a plan to prepare now for retirement.

_____

_____

_____

_____

_____

_____

_____

_____

_____

_____

_____

_____

_____

_____

_____

Bonus Information: The 2-2-2 Rule

What started as a thread on Reddit has gained attention for being a great idea and was even featured in an article for Good Housekeeping (Harvey-Jenner, 2019). A couple established a rule that:

Every 2 Weeks, they'd go out for the Evening.
Every 2 Months, they'd go away for the Weekend.
Every 2 Years, they'd go away for the Week.

Though this timeline may not fit every couple's routine given financial differences and family obligations, it is a perfect example of having a game plan! Talk to your partner and decide on a similar idea that will work best for you and Stick With It!

#8

What chore would you prefer to avoid at all costs?

Make a plan of attack - together!

Would you rather go for a root canal than go grocery shopping? Since childhood, was cleaning the bathroom your chore, and you hate every second of still doing it? Your partner will be your teammate for life, so make a game plan that makes you both happy! This isn't the 1950s anymore: wives don't have to do all the cooking and other household duties while working full-time. Some people may be judgmental, but there are no cookie-cutter marriages anymore. Women can do yard work, and men can do household chores. It is better to divide and conquer the tasks!

This is especially important with children in the picture. You'll have to add the child-care duties to the game plan during their younger years, but it is healthy for children to see parents work together at home. Be the team you promise to be when you say "I Do." As children get older, you can pass chores on to them (not turning them into 'Cinderella' though.) By giving children age-appropriate tasks, you instill the importance of hard work and encourage respect for your home and belongings. Just make sure you aren't assigning chores based on gender bias.

Since it's the two of you now (and maybe forever), make a game plan and offer to take on the chore your partner absolutely hates! Both hate the same chore? Alternate months or do it together and find a fun reward you can share!

_____

_____

_____

_____

_____

_____

_____

_____

_____

_____

_____

_____

_____

#9

Do you have a vice? (Smoking, alcohol, gambling, porn…) Do you have any sexual expectations for your Married life? Also, what do you consider 'cheating?'

Your future spouse <u>should</u> already know this about you. If they don't, consider - why? Is there a reason you are hiding it from your partner? Now is the time to be honest and open, so there are no surprises once you live together. (Once married, don't let your spouse be 'surprised' to find these while cleaning or on the computer.)

Do you have any sexual expectations you wish to discuss now? You don't have to be intimate 'x' amount of times each week to have a long and happy marriage. Life gets busy and you are allowed to be tired or just not 'in the mood.' You want quality over quantity in your time together. Discuss how you each feel about frequency and any expectations you may have had in mind.

Also, what do you consider 'cheating,' and how would a breach of trust be resolved? Do you want to have strict communication and want to know whenever your partner interacts with anyone? Or are you planning on having an Open Marriage? (Both options – and everything in between – is fine for a committed couple to decide, as long as that decision is made together.) Define 'cheating' as a team and set boundaries that align with your personal and religious beliefs.

If you are planning to have an Open Marriage, be sure to define the rules and create a game plan together. This ensures that you are both physically and emotionally safe. Creating your own rulebook also prevents an open interaction from evolving into cheating. Include rules like safe sex practices, location boundaries, how to select the other person, and regulations on what you can do or say to the other person.

_____

_____

_____

_____

_____

_____

#10

How do you like to vacation? Exotic? Staycation? Camping? What about weekends? How will you balance 'we' time & 'me' time?

Just as you view success, you want to make sure that you are both on the same page when it comes to downtime. People work hard for vacations, and you want to both enjoy it. If one person loves to go camping and get away from everyone and the other wants to travel and meet new people, there will be conflict whenever vacation time comes around. Discuss your preferences now if you haven't already. Also, if one partner is a housewife - or house spouse, make sure that you both agree to vacation options. Household chores are still hard work, and both partners need a break from routine. If you won't be taking vacations often due to finances, create a plan for a specific anniversary. This will give you both something to look forward to and have fun planning!

As with vacations, you both work hard all week and need to decide your expectations for weekends. If one person wants to sleep in on the weekends and the other wants to be out early and make the most of their forty-eight hours off, there will be hostility and arguments down the road. Decide on expectations now. Is 'Sunday Night Football' non-negotiable or are there certain games you'll want to watch? Do you have established salon appointments that you want to keep? Also, keep in mind that you and your spouse may have different days off. You are both hard-working, and self-care is essential. Let your spouse know what you need, and they can help you enjoy your day off, as long as you help them in return. (Expectations for future children's schedules need to be discussed as well. What elements of your routine will be most important to continue? Will you both be willing to adjust your routines once ballet lessons and soccer games are included in the schedule?)

_____

_____

#11

Are there any family secrets you've yet to reveal? How will you be caring for your families in the future? Also, establish health decisions for your partner & yourself.

You and your partner need to discuss any family secrets - information either of you may have been reluctant to share with anyone you previously dated. Being Engaged, you both need to know what the future holds. Does a relative on either side have a history of gambling, drugs, alcohol, or domestic violence? Is there a chance your partner could be called at work if a problem occurs? You both need to be open and honest about these possibilities and expectations. A game plan should be set up for any possible issues.

It will also be helpful to realistically discuss worst-case scenarios and how you plan to tackle the situation - before the Marriage. If an illness unexpectedly occurs for a family member (or your partner's), will you be taking that family member in to live with you? How about when either of your parents, aunts, uncles, … are elderly and need extra assistance? Will they be moving in with you? (There is no judgment in asking this question, but it IS something that needs to be discussed.) Both of your feelings and opinions need to be validated, and an agreed understanding needs to happen before the Marriage. If your partner expects the world to stop for their family and won't do the same for yours, this will cause problems if something should happen. It is best to discuss options and scenarios now before the union is official. (It is also smart to discuss possible scenarios with siblings so that you all understand general expectations.)

Also (though this isn't the happiest topic), discuss how you and your partner would want to be cared for if either of you had a terminal illness or deadly accident. Does either of you want a DNR (Do-Not-Resuscitate), DNI (Do-Not-Intubate), or AND (Allow Natural Death)? Would either of you want to be on life support in the hospital for years? Let your partner know of your wishes now. Again - it's important, though unpleasant - to discuss creating a will (so your wishes *are in print) and set up or reassign life insurance policies after you are Married. Put the information in a safe and secure place where you both have access to it.*

_____

_____

_____

_____

_____

_____

_____

_____

_____

_____

_____

_____

_____

_____

_____

_____

_____

_____

_____

#12

What kind of couple do you want to become? Which marriages serve as an excellent example for yours? What kind of married couple do you hope to avoid becoming?

Simply, these questions will help set the tone for your Marriage. Discuss influences in real life and couples from books and the media. When you and your partner watch television or films, discuss the couple's obstacles in the storyline. Do you agree or disagree with their decisions?   How would you have responded differently?

Also, when obstacles do arise, how will you handle them? Being honest and direct is key to being a team. Agree now to come straight to your partner with any problems instead of telling other family members, friends, or venting on social media first. Most issues can be resolved quickly if you put your partnership first! Be fair and discuss how you would like handle disagreements.

_____

_____

_____

_____

_____

_____

_____

_____

_____

_____

_____

_____

_____

_____

_____

_____

_____

_____

Bonus Information:
Beware the Bridal Blues

It was very important to me that this be included in Section One. You need to know about this <u>before</u> the Wedding. While it doesn't happen for every Bride or Groom, it often strikes unexpectedly.

So what are the Bridal Blues? They are the deflated feelings and depression that can occur after your Wedding Day. According to Jocelyn Charnas, a clinical psychologist and premarital counselor, "[It] happens when couples experience a period of letdown following the excitement of planning the wedding." (Torgerson, 2018)

'Letdown' is a terrific definition of the Bridal Blues. You have been planning your Wedding Day for months (even years). Some may have started daydreaming/ planning it since they were tweens! Once the Honeymoon is over, reality sets back in, and daily life can feel dull and uneventful. I remember a similar realization after I was out of school and in the workforce. When you are in school, there are regular events to look forward to: dances, special holiday parties, random events,

*graduation ceremonies/ parties, school breaks, etc....
Adulthood is typically anti-climactic until there are these
major life milestones. Some of your guests may even
feel disappointed that your Wedding is over as it
provided an escape from the monotony of schedules.
Immediate families of both the Bride and Groom can also
feel disappointed once the planning is over.*

*However, no one feels the Bridal Blues more than
the Bride or Groom. There's no need to feel guilty over
these feelings either. Even though you had a wonderful
day and are now married to someone you love, you
aren't a selfish person if the disappointment sets in.
Heck, be honest - you may genuinely miss the spotlight!
That's completely fine, and you are not alone! Sage
Grazer, a licensed therapist and co-founder of Frame
Therapy, explains, "Your brain is quite literally returning
to a state of homeostasis, unwinding after a period of
heightened excitement, stress, anticipation, and energy."
(Muenter, 2021) See! There's a physiological
explanation for your feelings! If you have a history of
anxiety or depression, keep in mind that you could be
more susceptible to these feelings.*

So how do you prevent the Bridal Blues? The best way is to talk to your partner and make a game plan! Make a pact to keep a routine or activity from your Engagement an active part of your Married schedule. Don't forget that you are Newlyweds and (even if you lived together before) this is still a fantastic season - enjoy it! Find ways to add bits of romance to your daily life.

You and your partner can also plan to start a new project together when the Wedding is over. (My husband and I started this publishing company.) It is important to focus your energy on a new activity, whether large or small, together or individually.

Another element Weddings can bring is a bonding between your family and friends. Keep those bonds going! Create regular meet-ups with family and friends. Planning social events will give everyone something to look forward to!

#13

Where is 'Home Sweet Home'? Where do you want to live? Does your job have an impact on that dream?

This is very important to know about your partner. If one of you wants to stay in the town where you grew up and the other wants to move far away, there will be resentment and issues if this isn't resolved before you are Married. Also, will either of your jobs require you to move occasionally? Are you both willing to move for the other? Will you support one another - even if this means uprooting your whole family? If not, this needs to be discussed with your partner.

_____

_____

_____

_____

_____

_____

_____

_____

#14

How does your partner feel about social media? How long could you live without your cell phone?

These questions are essential for modern couples. Does your partner post everything about their lives on social media? Will you be comfortable with them sharing personal information? Do you want them to record everything, or do you prefer to live in the moment? Discussing this now will be better than having resentment later on. It's completely fine if both partners want to share every moment with the world - as long as they both agree. Discuss and create code words for when you prefer to keep moments private.

The same goes for gaming and simply being on their phone. Does your partner love to play games, or do they constantly seem to be scrolling on social media? There's nothing wrong with either, and it's a great distraction. However, time with your partner is important. Discuss preferences you both have and set limitations regarding phone time.

#15

How did your previous relationships prepare you for this one? What were the 'deal-breakers' that made you decide whom to date in the past?

You've probably already discussed previous relationships with your future spouse (should have). The twist is that we learn something from everyone in our lives. What lessons or experiences lead you to find your partner? Have you learned from the mistakes you may have made in previous relationships? If not, what is it that you need to work on? How can your partner help? Remind your partner how they ranked better than anyone else and how excited you are to spend your life with them!

_____

_____

_____

_____

_____

_____

This is the end of Section One! Yay!

Not feeling excited? Time to discuss any concerns with your partner and decide if moving forward is right for you.

Thrilled that you and your partner knew those answers already - and had interesting discussions along the way? Give your partner a high-five, a hug, or a kiss (or all three!)

Time for fun questions in the other sections! Sections 2 - 5 are full of great questions for getting to understand one another even better! (Some questions even make great conversation starters with family and friends!)

Think you and your partner know each other well? Make a game of it and guess your partner's answer!

Section Two:
Know Me Better!

What kind of person do you want to be?

_____

_____

_____

_____

_____

How do you want to make others feel?

_____

_____

_____

Are you jealous of anyone? Whom and when did you feel this way?

_____

_____

_____

_____

What's something you need to release from your life?

_____

_____

_____

_____

What represents home for you?

_____

_____

_____

_____

What makes you feel most peaceful?

_____

_____

_____

_____

How do you feel appreciated?

_____

_____

_____

_____

Where is your 'Happy Place' & why is it there?

_____

_____

_____

_____

What is a ritual or routine that you need to do every day or most days?

_____

_____

_____

_____

How are you most productive?

_____

_____

_____

_____

What makes you lose track of time?

_____

_____

What do you get bored of?

_____

_____

_____

_____

Do you believe in luck? Do you have a lucky item, number....?

_____

_____

_____

_____

How would you like to celebrate the best birthday ever? Has it happened already, or is that how you wish to commemorate a particular age? Do you enjoy surprise parties or prefer to be part of the planning process?

_____

_____

_____

_____

What career goals or dream jobs do you have? What's your inspiration?

_____

_____

_____

_____

Do you want to go back to school for anything?

_____

_____

_____

_____

Regardless of whether you already have one, what is a tattoo you would want & where would you put it?

_____

_____

_____

_____

What gives you strength during challenging times? How do you recharge yourself?

_____

_____

_____

_____

What is the best advice you have ever received?

_____

_____

_____

_____

Are you trying to break a bad habit right now? How can your partner help?

_____

_____

_____

_____

What's the moment that you are most proud of?

_____

_____

_____

_____

What's the best compliment you've received (not from your partner)?

_____

_____

_____

_____

Do you have confidence in yourself? Why or why not?

_____

_____

_____

_____

_____

If you won ___ amount of money, what would you do with it?

_____

_____

_____

_____

Do you have a prized possession? Why that item?

_____

_____

_____

_____

Of all your partner's friends, who is your favorite & why?

_____

_____

_____

_____

Do you think aliens exist? What do you think they'd be like compared to aliens in movies, books, or pop culture?

_____

_____

_____

_____

Are you having trouble getting along with anyone right now? Who & why?

_____

_____

_____

_____

Of all the colleagues you've had, whom do you miss working with the most?

_____

_____

_____

_____

What makes you feel at your best? A particular environment, specific people, etc......

_____

_____

_____

_____

Is there a skill you would like to master? Perhaps you and your partner can learn it together?

_____

_____

_____

_____

What 'boggles your mind' or completely dumbfounds you?

_____

_____

_____

_____

Whom would you pick if you could have dinner with one person (living or dead)?

_____

_____

_____

_____

What's the one item you always keep with you? Why that object?

_____

_____

_____

_____

_____

What is your favorite time of day & why?

_____

_____

_____

_____

Be completely honest: how do you feel about aging?

_____

_____

_____

_____

What annoys you, or is your pet peeve? What makes you cringe?

_____

_____

_____

_____

What is your guilty pleasure that brings joy to your life?

_____

_____

_____

_____

_____

What kind of gifts do you like best?

_____

_____

_____

_____

How much sleep do you need? How do you fall asleep when you can't? What position do you usually sleep in? Do you prefer to sleep warm and bundled up, or do you like to sleep with the cold air and fan on high?

_____

_____

_____

_____

What food will you never eat? Why? (Not including food allergies.)

_____

_____

If you could have any job, what would it be? What job would you never want?

_____

_____

_____

_____

What life decisions would you have made differently?

_____

_____

_____

_____

What movie, book, show, or song do you feel is overrated?

_____

_____

_____

_____

What's the best practical joke played on you? (The worst?)

_____

_____

_____

_____

What's a riddle or joke you'll never forget?

_____

_____

_____

_____

Whom would you want to do the voice-over if your life was narrated?

_____

_____

_____

_____

When have you snooped or accidentally found something out that you wish you hadn't?

_____

_____

_____

_____

What's an interest of yours that you wish was more popular?

_____

_____

_____

_____

What's the funniest conversation you've overheard?

_____

_____

_____

_____

Would you rather be too hot or too cold? Does this have an impact on where you would like to live?

_____

_____

_____

_____

What songs provide nostalgia every time you hear them?

_____

_____

_____

_____

How did your parents meet?

_____

_____

_____

_____

What's something that everyone should be taught (or adults need to be retaught)?

_____

_____

_____

_____

Would you rather know how you will die, when you will die, or are you happy knowing neither?

_____

_____

_____

_____

What's the oldest item currently in your closet?

_____

_____

_____

_____

What's the weirdest gift you've received?

_____

_____

_____

_____

What's the worst-smelling location you have ever experienced?

_____

_____

What article of clothing represents you the most?

_____

_____

_____

_____

What movie or book would you like to exist in?

_____

_____

_____

What sound irritates you the most?

_____

_____

_____

_____

Do you like your name? If not, what would you want it to be?

_____

_____

_____

_____

What's something you used to enjoy but don't anymore? Why?

_____

_____

_____

_____

How comfortable are you with public affection? What part of your body do you love/ hate to be touched?

_____

_____

_____

_____

Bath vs. Shower! Which do you prefer? Also, do you sing in the shower? What songs do you typically sing?

Section Three:
Childhood Memories

You should know each other's birthday, but what TIME were you born?

_____

_____

_____

_____

Who was your celebrity crush? (As a kid, teenager, adult?)

_____

_____

_____

_____

Did you have a favorite/ least favorite subject in school?

_____

_____

_____

_____

What's the most important thing your parents or parental figures taught you?

_____

_____

_____

_____

What was your favorite toy? Do you still have it?

_____

_____

_____

_____

What is something you wish you had or did as a child?

_____

_____

_____

_____

Sharing is caring! Did you share easily as a child or had to learn to compromise? Are you still learning?

_____

_____

_____

_____

What similarities or differences are there in how you and your partner were raised?

_____

_____

_____

_____

Was there a favorite tv show, film, or book you loved? Did your partner love it too? Bonus: Are you able to find it online? Share it with your partner! Has it stood the test of time?

_____

_____

_____

_____

Who was your most exciting or influential teacher? Your worst?

_____

_____

_____

_____

Was there a favorite game from your childhood? Did your partner enjoy it too? Play together!

_____

_____

_____

_____

What chores did you have as a child? Did you have an allowance? Would you want your children to have one? Why or why not?

_____

_____

_____

_____

How has life been different than you imagined as a teenager?

_____

_____

_____

_____

As a child, what wild animal: real, extinct, or fictional, would you have loved to have as a pet?

_____

_____

_____

_____

What's the worst mistake you've made as a kid? Teen? Adult?

_____

_____

_____

_____

How did your family handle finances when you were growing up? What should you and your partner do differently?

_____

_____

_____

_____

What's the most expensive thing you've broken?

_____

_____

_____

_____

What's the silliest thing you remember getting upset about?

_____

_____

_____

_____

What did you think would be awesome as a child but isn't?

_____

_____

_____

_____

How did some of your families' traditions get started? Any fun stories behind them?

_____

_____

_____

_____

What's something you did that your parents still don't know about?

_____

_____

_____

_____

Section Four:
Imagine If...

...You are stranded on an island but get an infinite supply of one food, one television (playing one film on loop), and only one book; which would you want them to be?

What invention could you never live without! (In reality, would you like to invent something?)

_____

_____

_____

_____

...You find a magic lamp with a genie inside! He will grant you three wishes (individually or as a couple). What will you wish for? The genie also can see the future! What would you like to find out?

_____

_____

_____

_____

...If you could live during one time period, which would it be and where do you live?

_____

_____

_____

_____

...You are a SUPERHERO!

-What would your hero's name be? A new nickname you share with your partner, perhaps?

-What superpower would you love to have? Is there a downside to certain powers?

-What's the most heroic thing you've done in real life?

-What is your catchphrase? What would you want it to be? Is it something you can say in real life (like a mantra)?

-Who is your enemy or arch-nemesis? What powers do they have?

-Who is your favorite hero? Would you want to team up with them?

-Who is your favorite villain? How would you defeat them?

...The Pharaohs of Egypt were buried with items they'd need in the afterlife. If you were Pharaoh & had your own pyramid, what would be in it?

_____

_____

_____

_____

...What animal would you want to be?

_____

_____

_____

_____

...If you could ask an animal a question, which animal and what would you ask?

_____

_____

_____

_____

...What fictional character would you love to meet?

_____

_____

_____

_____

...What would you like to commute with if you could travel by any means (a horse & carriage, a flying car, a spaceship, etc...)?

_____

_____

_____

_____

...If you could read someone's mind, whose would it be? Why them?

_____

_____

_____

_____

...If you had to wear a Halloween costume every day for the rest of your life, which would you choose?

_____

_____

_____

_____

...If you could win any award, what would it be? Do you know what you would say in your acceptance speech?

_____

_____

_____

_____

Section Five:
Couples' Bonding

How has your partner changed you for the better?

_____

_____

_____

_____

What is a small random thing your partner does that makes your day?

_____

_____

_____

_____

Who would play you and your partner if a movie were made about your relationship?

_____

_____

_____

_____

What's your families' medical history? This is information you'll need to know at doctors' appointments for the rest of your life! Get the information now! Create a credit card-sized list of the medical histories for each of you. Laminate them and keep them in your wallets for easy access and emergencies.

_____

_____

_____

_____

What is your personal theme song? What's yours as a couple? (It could be an idea for your first dance!)

_____

_____

_____

_____

What's a sexual fantasy you and your partner can fulfill together?

_____

_____

_____

_____

Do you know your star signs? Are your signs compatible? Do you believe them?

_____

_____

_____

_____

How will you celebrate your First Anniversary?

_____

_____

_____

_____

Design your dream home together! No architecture degree is required! Cut and paste photos out of magazines or get some paper and pencils and get creative!

_____

_____

What would the title be if a book was written about your relationship?

_____

_____

_____

_____

Will you be sharing the same last name? Whose will it be? If you have children, whose last name will they use?

_____

_____

_____

_____

Do you have a prediction about your future? What goals do you share?

_____

_____

_____

_____

Create a bucket list together!

_____

_____

_____

_____

_____

Should toilet paper hang over or under?

_____

_____

_____

_____

Who were you most excited to introduce your partner to?

_____

_____

_____

_____

Which celebrity does your partner remind you of?

_____

_____

What are your top favorite movies of all time? Haven't seen your partner's choices? Watch together!

_____

_____

_____

_____

Would you & your partner love to play a sport together? Take dance classes?

_____

_____

_____

_____

If you plan on having children, what would you like to be similar or different from how you were raised?

_____

_____

_____

_____

What is your dream vacation? Is it your Honeymoon? Is there a special occasion you would like to celebrate on that particular vacation?

_____

_____

_____

_____

What most excites you about spending your lives together?

_____

_____

_____

_____

Create a goal as a couple! (Not career or children related.)

_____

_____

_____

_____

Design an awesome obstacle course together!

_____

_____

_____

_____

Do you have a name for your car (or another object)? Make one up together!

_____

_____

_____

_____

If there was a soundtrack to your life, what songs would be on your album? Make a playlist together!

_____

_____

_____

_____

Do you know what each other's names mean? If not, look them up together!

_____

_____

_____

_____

What do you have difficulty talking about? Make a promise to be non-judgmental and helpful with one another as you find solutions to problems.

_____

_____

_____

_____

Here's to Your 'Happily Ever After'!

Thank you for reading this book! I hope it was informative, entertaining, and helpful to both of you! You can even go over the questions every Anniversary and see how your answers change over time! (There are extra blank pages after the 'Resources' section.)

My husband and I have been together for over a decade (maintaining a strong long-distance relationship for several years in that time). My parents are celebrating their fabulous 40th Anniversary this year! We have all had different highs and lows in life, but we've relied on one another. The most important key to being a successful couple is honesty and depending on your partner when you need it the most. Always be there for your teammate and partner in life!

I know the term 'Happily Ever After' gets mocked because every day is not always happy. However, the point is for the number of days filled with joy to outnumber the ones filled with sorrow. With this in mind, as long as you marry someone you truly love and maintain communication and honesty with one another, I hope you indeed have a 'happily ever after' of your own!

May you become the couple others look to for inspiration. Enjoy the rest of your Engagement season and your transition into Newlyweds and being a Married Couple! I hope you and your partner have a wonderful and strong relationship that continues to grow long into your Marriage!

If you found this book helpful, please leave a review where you purchased it! This will help other couples find it and help them prepare for their 'Happily Ever After' too!

Resources:

100+ fun relationship questions for couples. PsyCat Games. (2021, December 22). https://psycatgames.com/magazine/conversation-starters/100-questions-for-couples/

200 questions for couples. Conversation Starters World. (2021, September 27). https://conversationstartersworld.com/questions-for-couples/

500 juicy and romantic truth or dare questions for couples. Relationship Culture. (2021, October 1). https://relationshipculture.com/truth-or-dare-questions-for-couples/

Ariane Resnick, C. N. C. (2021, December 9). *How to have a successful open marriage.* Verywell Mind. Retrieved March 17, 2022, from https://www.verywellmind.com/how-to-have-an-open-marriage-successfully-5204975

Bible Hub. (n.d.). Proverbs 20:3. Retrieved April 1, 2022, from https://biblehub.com/proverbs/20-3.htm

Brown, L. (2021, December 15). *201 questions for couples that will bring you closer together.* Hack Spirit. https://hackspirit.com/questions-for-couples/

Burke, Z. (2021, August 24). *The 31 things you should definitely discuss before marriage.* Weddings. https://www.hitched.co.uk/wedding-planning/organising-and-planning/what-to-discuss-before-marriage/

Chase, A. (2020). *One question a day for newlyweds: A Journal for the first year of Marriage.* ST MARTIN'S Press.

Daly, A. (2021, November 1). *Why getting depressed after your wedding is such a thing.* Cosmopolitan. Retrieved February 25, 2022, from https://www.cosmopolitan.com/lifestyle/a27275386/post-wedding-depression/

Davenport, B., Collins, S., & Houghen, W. (2021, July 30). *77 questions for couples guaranteed to ignite amazing conversation*. Live Bold and Bloom. https://liveboldandbloom.com/09/relationships/questions-for-couples

DNR/DNI/And: CureSearch. CureSearch for Children's Cancer. (2021, October 19). Retrieved March 27, 2022, from https://curesearch.org/dnr-dni-and

Frye, D. (2020, November 23). *Why pregnancy and birth terrify certain people*. Psychology Today. https://www.psychologytoday.com/us/blog/finding-balance-postpartum/202011/why-pregnancy-and-birth-terrify-certain-people

Harvey-Jenner, C. (2019, June 17). *This could be the secret to keeping your relationship fresh*. Good Housekeeping. Retrieved March 27, 2022, from https://www.goodhousekeeping.com/uk/news/a557300/secret-fresh-happy-relationship-2-2-2/

Housespouse. Urban Dictionary. (2009, October 7). Retrieved March 27, 2022, from https://www.urbandictionary.com/define.php?term=housespouse

Jasper. (2021, December 23). *98 fun questions for couples - spark fun conversations*. Mantelligence. https://www.mantelligence.com/fun-questions-for-couples/

Jones, C., Wadephul, F., & Jomeen, J. (2021, August 25). *Tokophobia: What it's like to have a phobia of pregnancy and childbirth*. The Conversation. https://theconversation.com/tokophobia-what-its-like-to-have-a-phobia-of-pregnancy-and-childbirth-91271

Martinez, J. (2017, November 17). *The Ins and outs of hysterectomies and Vasectomies*. Vanguard. https://psuvanguard.com/the-ins-and-outs-of-hysterectomies-and-vasectomies/

Movie Trailers Source. (2020, October 5). *The Expecting Official Trailer (2020)*. youtube.com. Retrieved from https://www.youtube.com/watch?v=pA8zTLajr5Q

Muenter, O. (2021, September 15). *Why doesn't anyone talk about post-wedding anxiety?* Brides. Retrieved February 25, 2022, from https://www.brides.com/why-doesnt-anyone-talk-post-wedding-anxiety-5195986

Nelson, J. (2020, July 28). *150+ best questions for couples to ask each other [2020].* Thought Catalog. Retrieved January 8, 2022, from https://thoughtcatalog.com/january-nelson/2020/07/questions-for-couples/

Ogletree, K. (2018, May 22). *10 important things every couple should do before getting married.* Real Simple. Retrieved March 15, 2022, from https://www.realsimple.com/work-life/family/relationships/things-to-do-before-marriage

Pawlowski, A. (2019, September 3). *9 things a couples therapist wants you to know before getting married.* TODAY.com. Retrieved March 13, 2022, from https://www.today.com/health/what-know-getting-married-couples-therapist-advice-t122403

Prisco, J. (2014, October 13). *Post-Wedding Depression is a Real Thing.* ABC News. Retrieved February 25, 2022, from https://abcnews.go.com/Lifestyle/post-wedding-depression-real-thing/story?id=26113769

Strauss, A. (2019, September 18). *From wedding bells to wedding blues.* The New York Times. Retrieved February 25, 2022, from https://www.nytimes.com/2019/09/18/fashion/weddings/from-wedding-bells-to-wedding-blues.html

Tocophobia (tokophobia): What is it and how to treat this? International Forum for Wellbeing in Pregnancy. (2018, June 23). Retrieved January 25, 2022, from https://www.ifwip.org/tocophobia-tokophobia/?cn-reloaded=1

Torgerson, R. (2018, July 17). *The postwedding blues are actually a thing-here's how to deal.* theknot.com. Retrieved March 28, 2022, from https://www.theknot.com/content/post-wedding-blues-tips-for-dealing

Vincenty, S. (2021, November 2). *25 questions to ask before you get married.* Oprah Daily. Retrieved March 13, 2022, from https://www.oprahdaily.com/life/relationships-love/a34427583/questions-to-ask-before-marriage/

Zlotnick, S. (2021, December 21). *73 deep conversation starters for couples.* Brides. Retrieved January 8, 2022, from https://www.brides.com/deep-conversation-starters-for-couples-5210683

Extra Pages:

www.ingramcontent.com/pod-product-compliance
Lightning Source LLC
Chambersburg PA
CBHW032101020426
42335CB00011B/439